Colors of Paradise

Colors of Paradise

a spiritual journey by

Fereidun Shokatfard

Library of Congress Cataloging in Publication Data
Library of Congress Control Number: 2005907673

Shokatfard, Fereidun
Colors of Paradise
Copyright ©2005 by Fereidun Shokatfard

Summary: A collection of poems and paintings, a spiritual journey

Printed in Korea

Publisher: Fereidun's
1600 Cabrillo Ave.
Torrance, CA 90501

ISBN 0-9772462-0-5

This book is dedicated to those who are making peace a reality

and contributing to the communication between nations, communities and people.

We are as different
as colors of the rainbow
What makes us illuminate
is the oneness of all colors
that let us be the shining light

Acknowledgement

I wish to acknowledge my wife Rika for her support and encouragement and believing in my creative and spiritual path. Her dedication for the cause of this book has helped me to excel.

I wish to thank Mr. Mehrdad Pahlbod, the former Iranian Secretary of Art and Culture, for his encouragement and for urging me that I should share my work with the world.

I salute my friends who gave me support and patiently waited for me to come through with the publication of my work.

My further gratitude goes to Ms. Sharon L. Lacey and Christina E. Forshay for helping me with the creative suggestions, graphics and technical support.

Introduction

Quite frankly, I have a difficult time describing the style of my paintings and writings. For the last several years, I questioned whether I should publish this book. What began as notes to myself, in form of paintings and writings almost eighteen years ago, took on a life of its own somewhere along life's journey.

My paintings are expressions from deep within. They are in watercolor, ink and acrylic. I use brush as well as tassel and string to paint. Tassel and string, by virtue of their uncontrollability, forces one to let go and not seek perfection. What I express when I let go of the fear of rejection, is coming from within, from my soul. I tried to minimize the controlling aspect of using the brush to give the tassel and string the upper hand so to speak.

When I reflect on my writings, there were days when I felt pretty good about what my soul expressed, but whenever I read Rumi, Hafiz, Saadi, Goethe, Neruda and other poets and teachers of love, I became doubtful of being adequate to share my writings with others. However, I have decided to share them with you as enhancements for my paintings.

For so many years, I felt I was standing on the edge of a cliff, wondering if I should dare to jump, hoping for a safe landing. If my work touches your heart, I made a safe landing and the jump was worthwhile.

Fereidun Shokatfard

Messenger

I have been many people
many times
At times a messenger
At times the message

Colors of Paradise
are endless dreams,
mingling souls…
In those colors
you would be
who you want to be
Colors are feelings
feelings are colors
all matching
New-comers are welcome
just wear a color and come in
Colors of happiness,
illuminating love,
where God is present

Colors of Paradise

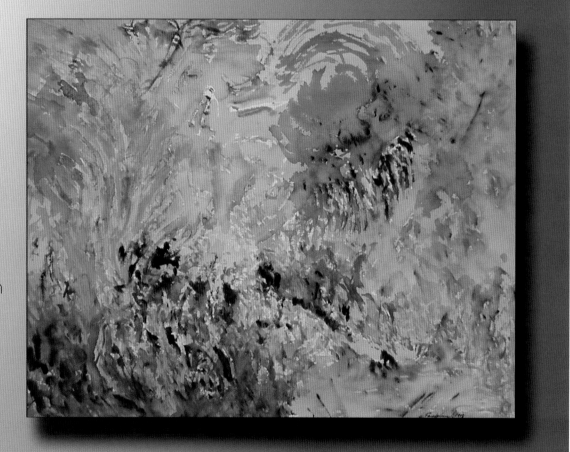

Call Me

Call me,
when I need
to be present
Talk to me,
when I am sad
Encourage me,
when I am in despair
Guide me,
when I am lost
Love me,
when I don't act loving
Be a friend

Spring Beneath the Tree

Spring beneath the tree
The nightingale whispers
to the rose
It has your name on it…
Has the color of
your blush,
The softness of
your feelings,
The innocence
of your soul

The Beginning

This is the beginning of
what is about
to come
and the end of
what has been
What it was,
is on another page
yet, you may read it
between the lines

Valley of Dreams

Walk with me
in the valley of dreams
Let us follow
the footsteps of
kings and peasants
to the tune
of eternity
See the grand
entrance of God
that we are all equal

Life is a Journey

Life is a stage
Suspended
between phases of consciousness
All the goods it has to offer
we can take it alone
or share it with others
in endless bliss

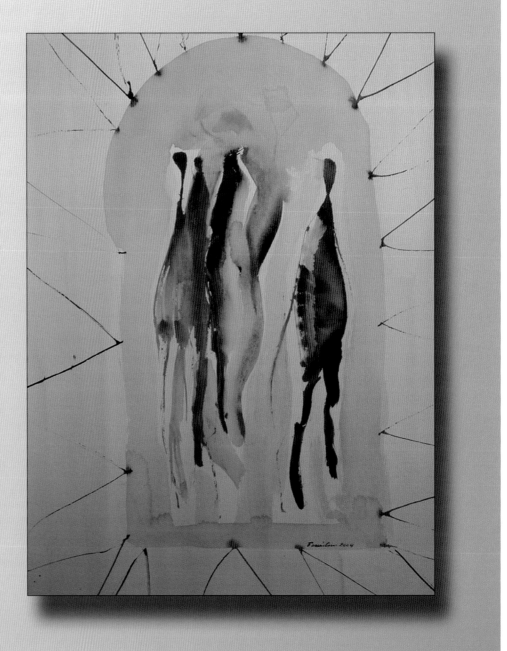

Tell Me

Tell me that love returns
when I open my heart again
that anger will vanish
so will the hurt and pain
Tell me I should be strong
ready for better times ahead
Tell me that every peak
is followed by a valley
and every valley
is joined by its peak
Tell me, I am still good
worthy and wonderful
even if I feel lost
Tell me that I should
tell myself all I have asked
you to tell me

Journey

With my mind
I soared with
the eagle of faith
to the summit of heaven
With my heart
I dove into the deepest
ocean of doubt
To always find
heaven and earth within

Light Within

The riches of a man's soul
is the light within the heart
Open the door
Let the light shine in
What use is it to invite the divine
love
and refuse the entry

Far Away Dream

Sky splashed with
birds heading south
Take me with you to the sun
Take me to far away places
Let me fly with the wind
beneath your wings
The sun in my face
and the joy of destiny
I want to talk to the
moon at sunrise
Walk to the edge of the lagoon
Listen to the thousand stories
of the butterfly
Take me to places
where I have been
when I was just a dream

Below the Rainbow Arch

Below the Rainbow Arch
are places I have been
some only in my dreams
My soul keeps wandering
in search of hidden music
Play me one more time
the rhapsody
of lover's dreams
Send me to far away places
and the front porch
of my house

A Place to Be

If I ever come to Shiraz
I would kneel and kiss the ground
If I could talk to the wind
I would send Hafiz my love
If I could get close to the moon
I would polish it to see the mighty
Damavand more clearly
If I would be burned

my ashes to be placed

on a mountain
Carried by the morning breeze
to the Caspian sea

Hand me the cup of dreams
to take one more sip
from the sweet sour wine of life
Pass it to others
They too, may want to forget
Don't kill the light
still glowing in my heart
My soul is dancing
with the myth of happiness
to the tune of a
fluttering butterfly, called hope
Don't ask me where I am
I am lost too
but I tell you , who I am
as soon as I find myself
in my wandering dreams

Beyond Here and Now

Crossroad

Like galloping dreams
in twilight
I reached the crossroad
which one to take?
I am wondering
if I should take
the easy way out
or the hard way in

Tavern

Leave the door open
Don't kill the light
Let everyone in
Don't ask where they came from
Some are here from the darkness
Some from the emptiness
Some arrive drunken
burning like a torch
dancing...
Wine bearer
Fill the cup for everyone
Don't kill the light
they belong with us

The House

They are still talking
Tomorrow I will listen
after the sun has set forever
I was in the house
An empty place
Let us build one with love
No doors, no ceilings
The time of prayer
is every time you open your

heart

The Right To Be

What is it about?
It is about unsaid, unfelt, untouched
It is about the unseen and unforgettable
It is about the vast hidden within
It is about the endless without a beginning
It is about the mind that can't grasp
It is about the heart that always yields
It is about you and I, and the rest of us
It is about the one who is not even a dream
It is about tomorrow that was yesterday
It is about the past still far ahead
It is about peace and healing of the souls
It is about forgiveness and gratitude
It is about the life we live
It is about the right to be

Just a Dream

I am reaching out
to reach the unreachable
To touch
the untouchable
I am riding a dream
That, like a wild mustang,
is untamable
Like clouds
caught in the current
spread all over the blue sky
Like shredded laces
Dreams fading in oblivion
Not much left of me
Not a dreamer
Just a dream

Weeping Statue

In another time
I was crowning a column at Persepolis
holding the roof
I have witnessed the celebration of Nouruz,
beginning of spring
I saw gatherings of kings, warriors and people
from all over the world
I have seen respect for one another and tolerance
I have seen love and justice
One night when the fire raged through the palace
I tumbled to the ground where I lay
for thousands of years covered with sand
When they dug me out from the darkness
nothing looked familiar
New monuments, people dressed in black
covered head to toe
The only familiar sound was the shepherd's flute
I couldn't help myself, but to cry
for the lost dreams

Life's Purpose

Life is not a race
It is not about who
runs the fastest or futhest
and who wins the trophy
Winners are strollers
who pick up
hugs and kisses
on the roadside
along the life's journey

Holding the Sun

Holding the sun
from setting...
Is it to keep the joy of now
or the fear of the unknown
that tomorrow brings?
Is it the light of the present
or the darkness that follows?
I will let go, if you ask me
and watch with you
the wandering spirit

Before Time Arrived

Oh Sun, the Moon, the Stars
When did we part
Oh, blush of the Lilac
Lavender Butterfly
when did you leave me
Whispering Willow, Prairie Grass
when did we become separated
Each of you
carries a piece of me
as I am carrying a piece of you
from inception
Before time arrived

Blessings

Walk in the path of your heart
if you seek ecstasy of love
Blessed those who dance
to the hidden music
Burn slow and deep
without the need to
set the world on fire

Fanfare of Silence

Listen to the fanfare of silence
Listen to the story of ego
Rulers and peasants
are all dust
Using the old dust
for the new mix
New monuments, new egos
which will turn to dust
Where is love? I ask
It may be buried beneath
the ego
or caged in oblivion
Go stand in the doorway
look out and listen
The wind is whispering
the melodies
of a shepherd's flute
of yesterday's dreams

When the Sun Lingers

When the sun lingers
I see a piece of you
as I have imagined it
A tranquil place
somewhere in my dreams
where passing time
has ceased to exist
where beauty is in being
I see you in every light
I feel you in every shadow
This is a sanctuary, a refuge
as it is a reflection of your soul

I am Love

I am the world
you are looking at
I am the sun
I am the moon
I am the weeping willow
I am the beauty showing myself
in the colors of the rainbow
And I am the wind that makes
the Autumn leaves dance
I am the sky
And I am the ocean
I am the shower in spring
And I am love
For that ....
you have to close your eyes to see

South Gate of Heaven

Sitting on the South Gate
of Heaven
Watching…
Thinking they finally
got here
What have they brought
with them
Hope and expectation
of eternal life?
of good surroundings?
Meeting friends
and relatives?
Or just to love and
to be loved

as it was …
In heaven on Earth

Through the Eagle's Eyes

The eagle knows
today's sunset
is a promise of
tomorrow's sunrise
The eagle knows
the motion of the world
and the universe
To see far places
you need to soar
To see beyond today
and tomorrow
you need to raise your spirit

Happy Tree

On the sunny side
of the Garden of
Eden
I saw a happy tree
In its shadow
time was resting

Painting Birds

Painting birds is fun
Painting thousands and thousands
is funny
The next time when you feel lost
with nowhere to go
Try it,
They will lift you up…the birds
Have fun, be funny

Love and Ego

Ego, like an invisible wall
separates love from its source
Those who have arrived
at the doorstep of heaven
are not clinging to themselves
They simply surrender to love
knock at the door and enter

On Cloud Nine

I know you have been there
the imaginary place
on cloud nine
where happiness is
ever in bloom,
pain and suffering, unknown
This is a sanctuary,
where time rests
I often go there
in my wandering dream

Untitled

Racing against time
to say the unsaid and
still I am not finished
Suddenly I drown
in the ocean of humility
in silence
Ego surrenders
Colors dancing in eternal light

Paint Me Love

Paint me joy
I paint you tenderness
Paint me love
I paint you God
Just hold me
So we can paint tomorrow

Truth of an Eagle

As I felt soaring
toward the endless sky
I saw myself reflected
on the polished surface of the moon
I took a dive to hide from my own ego
Consciousness is our greatest bliss

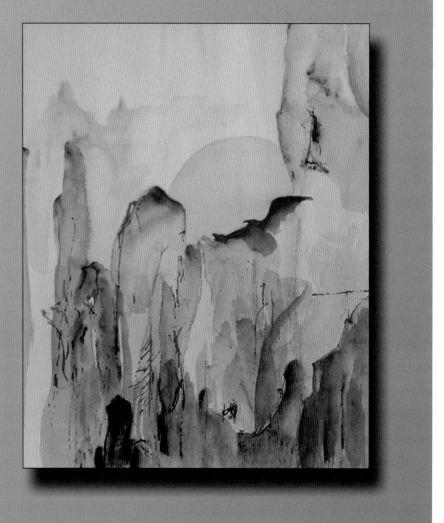

Somewhere in Time

Somewhere in time
they are still waiting
for a messenger to arrive
Who would be the messenger?
What would be the message?
Lovers are happy now
Blessed are those
who remember love

Lovers

Lovers are believers in oneness
For they are one
They are drowned
in the joy of now
The rest
are details

Joy of My Heart

The Joy of my heart
is the glow
of the rising sun
in your smile…
Words follow,
How wonderful
to be like the tree
that first flowers
then grows its leaves

When I am dreaming of the horsemen
who poured out
of my soul onto my canvas
I wasn't sure where they came from
Where they were going
I gave each one a piece of me
as a token of peace
I look and wonder
if they are still going
or coming back
They can keep me a while longer
I love to dream with them
as they are moving
with the speed of thunder
Sounds of hoofs
unite the souls of warriors
who are carrying my dream
I'll keep my heart
in the palm of my hand
as I stand high on the cliff
for them to find the way home

Destiny

Sundance

As I dance to the sun
I am dancing to the beat of the universe
which is aligned with the beat of my heart
With every step I get further away from me,
from my body
At the end my soul is dancing
I dare you to join in
this is the path to eternity

Flight of the Eagle

Within all of us
the eagle is
waiting to fly
Taking flight
takes time
For some
it takes a lifetime
Those who look
at their wings
and still believe
they can't fly,
Because they were told so
Freedom
if not by death,
comes by determination

House of God

I said, I am here
a promise to keep
You said promises are for those
doubtful of commitment
I said, what happened
to the glorious temple of might,
Your house
You said, buildings
are destined to decay
I said, I thought I was
to meet you here at sunrise
You said, the sun was always
shining in my heart
because
you never left me

The Man

The man with the golden heart
Built a golden carriage of goodness
It took him a lifetime to perfect it
In a warm summer day he was done
He called the butterflies whom he
raised
to pull his carriage to Heaven
in the gentle summer breeze
My father, the man we love

Toward the Unknown

Those days are gone
Children didn't have to
keep heads down
walking through the woods
Someone else wants
their home
"They" have a nobler blood
more rights
God's blessing
and plenty of guns
to prove it

You

A thousand doors open
yet you are invisible
Thousand stories are told
yet you are left to imagination
Those who yearn to connect
are lost and question
if they should look within
or find you above the clouds

Life is Being

Life is the seven colors
of the rainbow
Life is a blink of an eye
Life is wanting and not having
Having it and not knowing
you have it
Life is the illusion
of being here
The illusion of having been here
Life is question...
after question
The question of what it all means
Life is unfulfilled dreams
Regret of yesterday, hope for tomor-
row,
Joy of being alive,
Life is being

Breaking Away

The past is burning in a blazing fire
The dove of peace never flew over this land
God never was, not here
Present is a crossroad which reads
"In Peace" or "In Pieces"

Praising God

...God said I know myself
I don't need to be praised
I need to be loved
Love me with your deeds

Passing Through

I was passing through
bent like a question mark
under the weight of time
I didn't know where I came from
where I was going
I was just walking
because everybody else did
Suddenly I heard a voice
deep within my soul
Where are you going? the voice
asked
I am passing through, I replied
Going where?
I don't know, I said
Why don't you put down the bag of
blame
At least you can look up
and see where you are going
You may never want to carry
that weight again

Eyes That Won't Blink

Moments frozen in time
Emptiness that fulfills
Silent cry
stronger than the beat of a
drum
Eyes that won't blink
Truth whispered in the wind
beneath the eagle's wing
Eagle sores
Cry...
He is free

Angel Voices

Chorus of angel voices
Seemingly mute
My heart pounding
A void
Singing in my dream
the melody of love and despair
A chirping bird answers
Trees are listening
The picture is fading into the stars
I´m still hearing the chorus

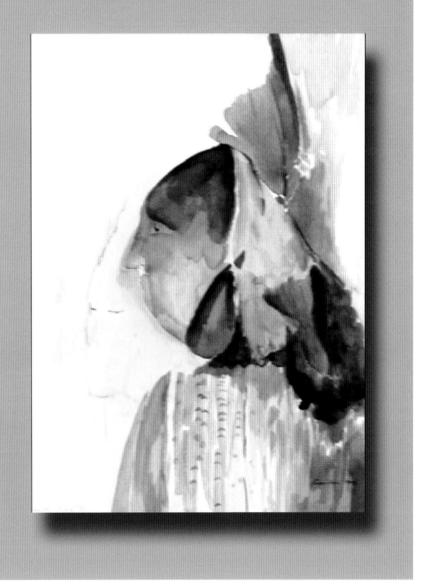

The Past

I like to remember
what some try to forget
The past…
I love those who taught me
and forgive those
who didn't know how to love

Boundless Dream

When you first came to visit me
I was absent
Yet I existed
in my ancestor's ashes
and in the glow of the sunrise
My mother was talking to me
when I was still in her womb
You were in your ancestor's ashes
And in the glow of the sunset
Yet destined to meet me

Dancing in a Thousand Lights

I don't have the humility
of the rosebud
that breaks its heart open
and shows its beauty
I am the silent stream
running quiet and deep
I do surrender to
the vast ocean
There, I will
dance in a thousand lights

Join the Dance

In the tavern of oneness
no one is sober
The wine of being
is in ever flow
Tell the holy man
to let go of ego
be silent
and join the dance

Who Is Love?

Searching in my scattered dreams
I feel the urge to go deep,
deeper than all colors
deeper than the ocean of nothingness
Which is the river, which is the
water rushing down the canyon?
Who is love?
who is the lover?
Who is hiding?
Who is seeking?
How can I look to find,
what I haven't lost?

Resting Point

I am still on my journey,
pausing just for a moment
The caravan left
while I was fast asleep
I may not catch up
if clouds of temptations
would cover the stars

A note long forgotten
by the writer,
Cherished, remembered
and placed for safe keeping
in a broken heart,
Revisited from time to time
when searching for the light,
buried in the memory
to see the sweet spot,
fading in silence
Clock ticking away
and the writer doesn't write any more
Nothing to write about
Feelings beneath the sand
and sand showing
the footsteps of time
Regrets, hope, and the new tide will cover it all
and no one will know
what was kept alive
hidden in the heart

A Note Long Forgotten

When Lavender Was Added

A pounding drum
resonates in my soul
Sends me to
distant past
and yesterday
when lavender was added
to the rainbow
I am searching
in the deepest corner
of my soul
for the sage and feather
of the eagle's wing
What else can I offer
when they open the gate
for my spirit to enter?

Off the Old Road

Happiness is…
walking through the woods
Just off the old road
Losing yourself in nature
Acting like a child again
Searching for
the greenest moss
and the four-leaf clover

I Love White Roses

They thought I was weird,
Delivering a flowering potted plant
to my father's grave
on Saturday mornings
and picking it up on the next
Thursday afternoon
You know, on Fridays
they would pick up and
discard all the flowers
I kept sharing my favorite garden flowers
with my dad
for years and years
My mom once told me
Son, it is funny what you are doing
It is has not been done before
But remember... I love white roses

Dance, Dance

When love seems beyond your reach

Dance, Dance, Dance

Like the dancing waves of the ocean

Your stillness is your demise

The Heartbeat of the Rose

Your voice
makes me tremble
Emptiness lingers
My head on your shoulder
Heart bleeding…
Come to me
Come with a whisper
No grandeur here
Just love
I will give you a white rose
color it with my blood
wear it on your chest
Feel the heartbeat of the rose
it is silent

When Dulcimer Talks

When words are unable
to tell the story
Dulcimer begins to talk
When a sigh freezes
in the chest
dreams are caged
Beauty beyond beautiful
can only be seen by the heart

A Moment to Remember

A Moment to remember
as it's always been
For a moment
For a life
With the urge
to join in
With desire
to be alone
Just you and I

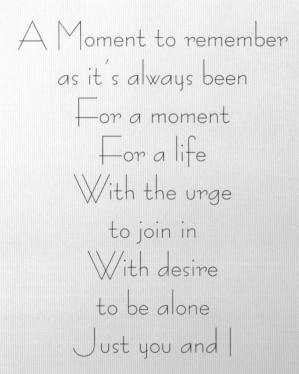

Picking Up the Pieces

Suddenly, you arrived
like a new page of poetry
calling me to wake up
and start to dream
in colors of love
Divine love…
The divine love can mend
all the broken hearts
you just have to give it
all the pieces

The Players

In the picture
I am the third one
from the left
and I see you
in the front row
And the rest of us
All players
What are we doing here?
Rehearsing life,
or playing it?
I forgot
if I am in front
or behind the curtain

Myth of Humanity

Acting as a human
a virtue
Looking like a human
a painting on the wall
Blessed are those
who choose love

over ego

To Life

To life
To letting go of regrets
To embracing the hope
To keeping your dream alive
To being the best you can be
To making a difference

Cause Unknown

The sight of dead Eagles
is a sight of sorrow
There were many of them
Many dead eagles
Many sights of sorrow
Once roaming the sky
Now, wings spread,
they are hugging the ground
Covered with mud
Some say they died of
lesions in the brain
"Cause Unknown"
They pollute the air, the water,
send waves of radiation
clear-cut the forest
rape the mother earth
and when asked…
Why the eagle dies?
They declare
"The Cause Unknown"

New Day

Sounds of nature in early dawn
Chirping birds greeting
the sunrise
Sun greeting back with
might and grace
Movement of people and beasts
Height of the rhapsody of nature
Joy, pain, sorrow, betrayal,
laughter, love, survival,
Life…
Phasing out the day
Resting…
Hope still lingering

I Believe

I believe in Goodness
I believe in Heaven on Earth
I believe in gratitude
and forgiveness
I believe in power of love
I believe in magic of a smile
I believe in healing of a hug
I believe in melting souls
I believe in you
I believe in me

Question

As far as I can see
I see you
even beyond unseeable
As far as I can think
I think of you
even beyond
the unthinkable
Is it me who is looking,
or is it you
who is shining?
Is it me
who is driven by intellect,
or is it you
who makes me think of love?

Gazing into Heaven

The Grandpa is gazing into heaven
to see the ultimate good life
He saw the sun shining, birds flying
A bunch of trees and a home
As in the painting by my son Bijan
when he was just five years old

If You Exist

From the sunrise of faith
to the sunset of doubt
to the secrets of heaven's gate
to nothingness,
the lingering question
if you exist
Love frightened of those thoughts
like a butterfly
in crashing waves
became the wings of the restless heart
seeking to escape
My soul looking, searching everywhere
if you exist...
...I found you
in a house of a friend
on the face of a child
in a cup of wine

Beat of Drums

Beat of drums
Elders watching
Pine needles looking down
Tree bark listening
Eagle soaring above
Majestic turn
around the fire
I am still holding
the tobacco in my hand
My turn will come
When I will sprinkle
it on the fire
As gesture of peace
Peace be with them
The brave Chumash Nation

Colors of Love

When I think of colors of love
I think of a piece of heaven
Where harmony overrides
The written words

Dancing

Dancing to the beat of the drum
our soul is dancing
Dancing to the beat of silence
we are the drummer

Who is Looking?

They are looking at me
through the bars
wondering why
I have been caged
True, bars are between us
The question is
who is in and who is out

Don´t Forget the Colors

Let us go back to
my town for a visit
This time I will take for them
some songs and vibrant colors
Sometimes I dive
into my own tears
Swim upstream all the way
to the beginning
You can come along
Just don´t forget the colors

Changing Times

Signs of changing times
This world got smaller
and smaller the hearts
More hatred, less love
More destruction, less healing
More I and Me,
less We and Us
And many claim to
have the truth
My heart aches
as the signs of suspicion linger
and no one asks
how much I can love

Invisible Destiny

The invisible hands of desires
Rearranging the moment
We know we can't
change the past
We think we can
change the future
The outcome was clear
from inception

The Third Eye

When the third eye looks
beyond the first layer of existence
the soul becomes speechless
What if someday
you look the great spirit
directly in the eyes
and all you see is yourself?

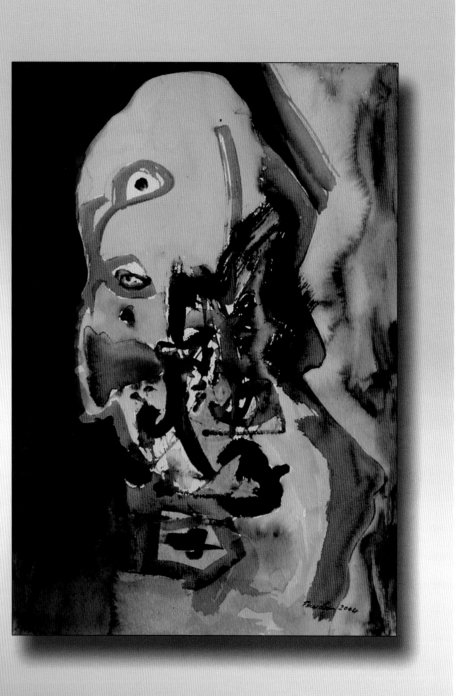

Caging Liberty

When the heart is open
it only retains goodness
Hatred is the attempt
of a closed heart
to cage the liberty
Trying to keep love
from blossoming
is like trying to rope
down a fluffy cloud

Starting Over

Beyond the thought
and imagination
you were alive in me
Before colors arrived
I saw you up in the air
from the airplane window
I tried to look far
but couldn't see
the end of eternity
I said, "God."
You said, "Son."
what happened to
your bewilderment?

Wisdom of the Heart

I left my heart
in a thousand places
and had to leave empty handed
You keep questioning my wisdom
Wisdom of the heart?
I am questioning your question

Life's Lesson

From all I have learned
I like to remember
the lesson of love and compassion,
The greatness of the human soul
Dignity to oneself
To go deep within and ask
Why am I here?
I want to sit, feel
and listen with my heart
My eyes closed
My ears shut, just to feel
I want to feel the depth of it all
and how far I can reach
Chores are distractions to
how far I can reach,
how life should be lived
Role models are few
and far between

With a Kiss

Behind this sky
behind the naked star
and further behind
you stand in front of me
as if I have gone full circle
yet I didn't move
and you remained untouched
Layers of blossoming thoughts
like bursting spring flowers
And I loose you between lavender
and a touch of burgundy
I am pressing the last star
in my hand
and throw it your way
with a kiss

Call It Destiny

Destiny, dancing ahead
in the valley of dreams
slipping into the mirror
as we play our parts
and call it destiny

I am the Child

I am the harp
Play me
I am the cup
Fill me
I am the star
Catch me
I am the fire
Rage me
I am the child
Love me
I am the love
Give me away

Place of Beauty

Looking for a place of beauty
is like looking for the perfect
rose
Which one is it?
Beauty is everywhere and nowhere
You recognize it
when you look at it
with your heart

Still Looking

Scattered thoughts
from being a cosmic dust
to the edge of imagination
to the Garden of Eden
and beyond....
Far beyond the endless
I promised to look for you
I am still looking

Footstep of Time

Stop...
Listen to the footstep of time
Dream...
Let us harvest
the umber grapes of love
before they fall
to the ground of reality
stepped on by passersby
holding the lantern of doubt
searching for the truth

Only Consciousness

Somewhere the
sun is rising
announcing a
new beginning
Somewhere the
sun is setting
declaring the end
of the day
The truth is
There is no beginning
There is no end
Only consciousness

Why Truth Matters?

Evolution or creation
God, nature or both
View points taken to extreme
to even kill for the point of view
Why does truth matter?
One man's answer
may be the other man's question
Unsharpen your senses
you may see the light
For now, I am whole
by the love of God

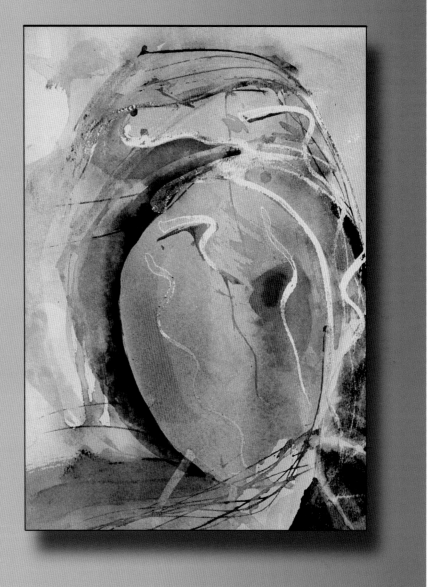

Magical Dance

Dance
Shape me with your magic
Shape me like a dream
vague and endless
Keep dancing…
We are amongst friends,
sinners, dreamers, and desperados
What use to close the door?
The Devil is already in

Too Excited To Sleep

Too excited to sleep
Too tired to get up
Have you had those moments
that you want to hug and kiss

everyone you meet
when life is beautiful
and being a bliss
Find out what happened
and make it happen again

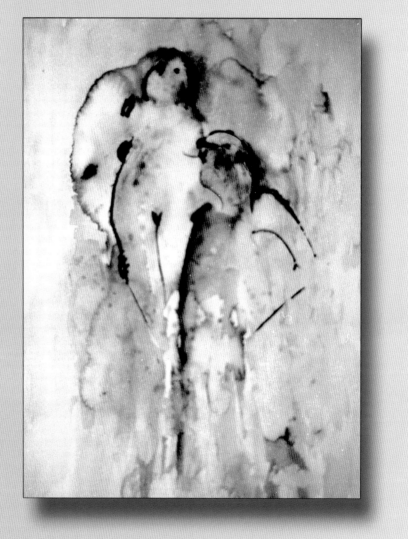

I am You

As if I knew where this path takes
me
I am on road for the longest time
you, whom I searched to find
found at last
I found you in me

Paintings with Stories

The following pages are dedicated to the events leading to some of my paintings or the discoveries I made long after I had finished certain paintings. I call each of these works a painting with a story.

Frequently, people ask me if I paint first, then write, or vice-versa. I actually do both. My paintings are done at chosen times, rather brief periods when I let myself go, allowing the colors to do their thing. In most of my paintings, I try not to allow my conscious mind to guide me. Sometimes words come as I am painting, or a verse captures me, occupying my mind until I see in it in colors.

When I met Gemma, a well-known artist, she greeted me at her door with an oxygen tube in her nose. She was 79, and not in good health. She greeted me by saying, "Son, I have been waiting for you all these years. Where have you been?"

We became good friends, and from time to time I attended her workshops. One day while visiting her, I came across a magazine from thirty years ago featuring Gemma and her work. I asked her if I could borrow it to make a copy for myself. She was delighted to grant my request. I took the magazine home with the intention of returning it quickly, but kept procrastinating, telling myself that I needed to return her magazine soon. Almost 2 month later, Gemma asked me for the magazine. Frantically, I searched for the magazine just to find out that it is had been thrown out with the morning paper. I didn't know what to do. Could I go to the dump to look for it? When was it dumped? I wasn't sure what to do, but knew, I was responsible. I was the only person to blame. I was looking for any possible way out of facing Gemma to tell her I had lost one of her prized possessions. I cried out to God, "Could you do me a favor and kill me on the spot? Would it be possible for the earth to open and swallow me or take my life in a car accident?"

Attempting to calm myself, I sat down to paint, painting birds on a piece of paper. Hours passed; I was in a meditative state, totally unaware of what was going on around me. Gradually, my painting comforted me. I knew I had to face Gemma. The next day, early in the morning, I went to her home. I saw her daughter, and briefly told her the story of my dilemma and showed her the painting with the birds. I asked her to tell her mother, that I would return shortly with some French pastry. When I returned, Gemma was standing in the doorway with her oxygen tube in her nose. This marvelous lady was crying as she said, son, I am so sorry to have caused you so much pain. I'm so glad you lost my stuff. How else would you have discovered how to meditate with art?"

Painting Birds

Eyes That Won't Blink

In 1993, I painted Eyes That Won't Blink. Like so many of my other paintings the image just appeared using tassel and string with accents done with a brush. What appeared is the face of an American Indian with a countenance that reflects incredible pain and suffering.

Nearly seven years later, I was driving home one day. Just before I reached my house, I had an uncontrollable urge to go back to Borders Bookstore. With little thought, I turned around and went back to the store. Upon entering, I went straight to a long table stacked with books. Picking up a book entitled: North American Indians, I saw the image of the man I had painted several years earlier. I discovered his name was Ishi, and he was an individual so well known that the public television ran a special about him. The book is written by Colin Taylor with a subtitle: A Pictorial History of the Indian Tribes of North America, published in Great Britain in 1997 by Parragon. I have been unsuccessful to obtain Permission from the publisher to print the picture of Ishi. You may look at it on Page 69.

I have often painted subjects connected to American Indians, but cannot explain the reason. One day after class in Germany, the professor asked me if I knew the meaning of my name Fereidun, pronounced Fe Ray doon. I answered that my name is that of a historic figure, an ancient king. He explained that my name has it roots in the Indo-German language, and in German, the meaning was Freier Donner. Translated into English, my name means Free Thunder.

The Man

My brother owned a Gift Gallery in Los Angeles, and my father, who was retired and in his early 80's, often hand crafted special articles for the shop.

Among his handmade items, there was one very special piece, a glimmering carriage made of copper and brass, pulled by five colorful butterflies with a clown as the driver. He spent hours and hours making sure every copper and colorful winged butterfly was perfect. He always said this particular piece represented his life story, his five children as the five butterflies, his very own butterflies that brought him to the United States from Iran, and provided him with a wonderful life.

When he took some of the sculptures to my brother's shop, this most popular design always sold quickly. After his passing, I found a Polaroid picture of his design, using it as an example for my painting, but showing him as the man, instead of the clown.

Cause Unknown

They found Derek, the son of one of my friends dead in front of the television. The cause was heart failure. He was only 32 years old. A few weeks earlier at his mother's house, I was showing him how to paint with tassel and string. He painted two images, each different and profound.

The same day as Derek's funeral, I read an article in the Los Angeles Times about the pollution that had killed many eagles, magnificent birds, that were found dead in the mud. At his funeral service, they displayed both his paintings. I kept looking at those paintings, silently asking "God, why?"

Later that day, after his ashes were scattered at sea and I returned home, I started playing with colors, thinking of Derek and the dead eagles. I finished the painting which I titled "Cause Unknown" and set it aside. Years later, I was looking at that painting, and was stunned to see Derek's face in it. His face was there, very clear and recognizable, as shown below. How did that come to be? I can't explain.

Follow the 2 markers on the sides. You will see Derek's face where the lines meet.

With a Kiss

My family celebrated my father's birthday on Father's Day. On a Father's Day after his death, I went to my dad's grave, but this time I felt a puzzling emptiness. It was not like other times when I felt he was resting there and I was talking to him like at his bedside. When I came home, I took out my materials and began painting. I had no clue what color to choose or what my objective was. In a semi-meditative state, I toyed with various colors. The result was the painting that I named "With a Kiss". I felt I located him there, somewhere amidst the scenery and vivid colors.